Notes on Prayer...

Elisabeth Elliot

GATEWAY TO JOY

P.O. BOX 82500
LINCOLN, NE 68501

Notes on Prayer . . .

First appeared in *Christian Herald* magazine.

Copyright © 1982 by Elisabeth Elliot
All rights reserved.

The Good News Broadcasting Association, Inc.
14,000 printed to date—1995
(1165-041—3.9M—95)
ISBN 0-8474-1192-3

Cover photo: Robert Cushman Hayes

Printed in the United States of America

Notes on Prayer...

People who ski, I suppose, are people who happen to like skiing, who have time for skiing, who can afford to ski, and who are good at skiing. Recently I found that I often treat prayer as though it were a sport like skiing—something you do if you like it, something you do in your spare time, something you do if you can afford the trouble, something you do if you're good at it. Otherwise you do without it most of the time. When you get in a pinch you try it and then you call an expert.

But prayer isn't a sport. It's work. As soon as I've said that, I'm in trouble because so many sports have become professional and as such are almost wholly indistinguishable from work. I could say that work is something you have to decide to do, you have to allow time for, you have to go at with energy, skill and concentration. But all those things could be said of the big business which is sports. Competition is deadly, equipment highly technical and expensive, salaries absurdly high.

But prayer is no game. Even if you are part of a "team," as when others join you in prayer, you are not cheered on by spectators or coached by any experts. You won't get any trophies—not on this side of the Jordan, anyway. It's not likely you'll get any credit at all. For some people prayer might fall into the category of "fun," but that's not usually the reason we pray. It's a matter of need and responsibility.

Prayer is work because a Christian simply can't "make a living" without it. He can't live a Christian life at all if he doesn't pray.

Prayer is the opposite of leisure. It's something to be engaged in, not indulged in. It's a job you give first priority to, performing not when you have energy left for nothing else. "Pray when you feel like praying," somebody has said. "Pray when you don't feel like praying. Pray until you do feel like praying." If we pray only "at our leisure"—that is, at our own convenience—can we be true disciples? Jesus said, "Anyone who wants to follow me must put aside his own desires and conveniences" (Luke 9:23, TLB).

The Apostle Paul did use an analogy from sports to describe prayer. He said we "wrestle." In the wrestling of a Christian in prayer, "our fight is not against any physical enemy: it is against organizations and powers that are spiritual. We are up against the unseen power that controls this dark world, and spiritual agents from the very headquarters of evil" (Eph. 6:12, *Phillips*). Seldom do we consider the nature of our opponent, and that is to his advantage. When we do recognize him for what he is, however, we have an inkling as to why prayer is never easy. It's the weapon that Unseen Power dreads most, and if he can get us to treat it as casually as we treat a pair of skis or a tennis racket he can keep his hold.

If we're going to ask, "*Is* prayer work?" somebody will want to ask, "*Does* prayer work?" That question assumes that results ought to be measurable. The trouble is they are not by any means always measurable or predictable because the One to whom we address our prayers is infinite and incomprehensible, "and all that is comprehensible about Him," wrote John of Damascus, "is His infinity and incomprehensibility." His thoughts are as much higher than our thoughts as the heavens are higher than the earth.

And He is Love. Infinite Love will never give a stone when bread is asked for, or a scorpion in place of an egg. But what will Infinite Love give if our prayer is for a scorpion?

Prayer is compared in the Bible to incense. "Let my prayer be counted as incense before thee," wrote the Psalmist, and the angel who stood before the altar with the golden censer in Revelation 8 was given incense to mingle with the prayers of the saints. Incense was very expensive, blended by a perfumer according to a strict formula. It appears to serve no particularly useful purpose. Its smoke and fragrance soon dissipate. Couldn't incense be done without?

Prayer is like incense. It costs a great deal. Sometimes it seems to accomplish little (as we mortals assess things). It soon dissipates. But God likes the smell. It was God's idea to arrange the work of the tabernacle to include a special altar for incense. We can be pretty sure He included all that was necessary and nothing that was unnecessary.

Christ prayed: He offered thanksgiving, He interceded for others, He made petitions. That the Son—coequal, coeternal, consubstantial with the Father—should come to the Father in prayer is a mystery. That we, God's children, should be not only permitted but commanded also to come is a mystery. How can we change things by prayer? How "move" a sovereign and omnipotent God? We do not understand. We simply obey because it is a law of the universe, as we obey other laws of the universe, knowing only that this is how things have been arranged: the book falls to the floor in obedience to the law of gravity if I let go of it; spiritual power is released through prayer.

I could say, "God can make my hands clean if He wants to," or I could wash them myself. Chances are God *won't* make my hands clean. That's a job He leaves up to me. His omnipotence is not impaired by His having ordained my participation, whether it be in the washing of hands with soap or the helping of a friend with prayer. Christ redeemed the world by the laying down of His life, a perfect sacrifice, once for all. Yet He is in the business, as David Redding says, of "maintenance and repair." He lets us participate with Him in that business by the laying down of our own lives.

One way of laying down our lives is by praying for somebody. In prayer I am saying, in effect, "my life for yours." My time, my energy, my thought, my concern, my concentration, my faith—here they are, for you. So it is that I participate in the work of Christ. So it is that no work of faith, no labor of love, no smallest prayer is ever lost, but, like the smoke of the incense on the golden altar, rises from the hand of the angel before God.